ONLY GOD
Could Do This

**The Ministry of
Jerome Wagenius**

ONLY GOD
Could Do This

The Ministry of
Jerome Wagenius

By Jerome Wagenius as told to
Ruth Denise Lowrie

ONLY GOD
Could Do This

Copyright © 2016 by Ruth Denise Lowrie

All rights reserved.

ISBN-13: 978-1537783505
ISBN-10: 1537783505

Christian Biography; Memoir

Published by Heart Outpourings Publishers
Des Moines, Washington

.

Table of Contents

PROLOGUE

Angry voices from the prison yard greeted Jerome and his Full Gospel team members as they entered the maximum security prison in Kigali, Rwanda. Only a thin barbed wire fence separated them from twelve hundred mass murderers crowding in front of them-- Hutu men who had participated in the one hundred day Genocide of 1994. Arranging a visit to this prison in 1996 was nearly impossible, because the government was sensitive about international publicity regarding those arrested, but by a miracle of God, permission had been granted.

The director of the prison explained that there had been a riot that morning, and as soon as the prisoners saw the team members approaching, anger turned from each other to the team. Cat calls and distorted faces of desperate, dirty men with scant clothing, were all the team could hear and see. Clenched fists and glaring eyes portrayed intense hatred and fear in the prisoners. As they looked at those men, guilty of despicable torture and murders, they began to realize God's unconditional love was much deeper than they had previously believed.

Rwanda is a tiny country in the heart of Africa. It is surrounded by Uganda, Zaire (the Democratic Republic of Congo), Tanzania and Kenya. Kigali, located in the middle of the country, is the capital city of Rwanda.

In this genocide an estimated eight hundred thousand innocent Tutsi men, women and children were brutally slaughtered with machetes, clubs, blunt objects and rifles by their Hutu neighbors and army units. The Hutus' objective was to eliminate the Tutsi tribe---rape, maim, murder, destroy or steal their property. Hutu gangs searched out and murdered victims hiding in churches and school buildings. Local officials and government-sponsored radio incited ordinary citizens to kill their neighbors. Those who refused to kill were often murdered on the spot.

The Rwandan Patriotic Front attacked the genocide perpetrators, and were eventually victorious. In those battles, many Hutus were arrested or killed. Genocide trials began in August of 1996. The Rwandan judicial system had been nearly destroyed, and the judicial process moved very slowly. An estimated one hundred thirty thousand men were held in inhumane Rwandan prisons. The Central Kigali prison, which Jerome's team visited in 1996, was one of those prisons.

"Oh Lord," they silently prayed. "Protect us. Keep us. Anoint us. We need You as never before. We are just ordinary people, but You can enable us to minister to these men before they face execution. Give us the words to say. Heal them emotionally, physically and spiritually."

They knew that only God could do this.

AUTHOR'S NOTE

The Full Gospel Business Men's Fellowship International (FGBMFI) is not a church, but one of the largest Christian business organizations in the world. In 1953, God gave Demos Shakarian a vision to be a storehouse of blessing for the whole world. "Our mandate from God is to break the chains of bondage in the world, to destroy the isolation of loneliness, and to link the world to God." Demos' vision was for Christians to be "the happiest people on earth."

Demos passed away in 1993, but his son, Richard Shakarian, is still carrying on the vision, and is the current president. "It is our destiny to lift up Christ in every business center and university . . . every nation, city, town and crossroads of the world." There are chapters all over the world, businessmen meeting in informal settings over a meal, and taking trips, called Airlifts, to nations across the globe to spread the message of Christ and encourage Christians worldwide. (The Full Gospel Business Men's Fellowship website (http://www.fgbmfi.org)

Jerome Wagenius made several airlifts with the FGBMFI from 1972 to 2000. One team member described his ministry as "Jerome's graceful; healing ministry." He also made personal trips after contacts in various countries called him back. He travelled through the U.S. two or three times a year, and once a year to other countries. In all Jerome made thirty-five world missionary trips. Many times his wife, JoAnn Wagenius, travelled and ministered with him. The chapters in this book are composites of trips he made: each country represents more than one trip to that area. In addition to the countries in this book, Jerome ministered in Japan, Honduras, Philippines and Mexico.

In the 1990's he travelled frequently throughout the U.S. with Bob Bignold, former president of FGBMFA (Full Gospel Businessmen's Fellowship in America) encouraging chapters and establishing new ones.

In 1998 the FGBMFI honored Jerome and JoAnn with a plaque which reads:

Inducted into the Pacific Northwest
HALL OF FAITH
Of
The Full Gospel Businessmen's
Fellowship International

Jerome & JoAnn Wagenius
27 November 1998

Who were called, chosen, and found
faithful in the ministry
Of the Full Gospel Business Men's Fellowship
International.
By faith they walked worthy of their calling,
kept the unity of the spirit,
equipped and released others to the work of the
ministry, and went to the nations with
the Good News of Jesus Christ.
By faith they demonstrated an
understanding of the times,

gave generously of their life and substance,
and overcame the world by the Blood of the Lamb
and the word of their testimony.
A couple who through faith have obtained an
eternal testimony and a place in the Pacific
Northwest Hall of Faith of the Full Gospel Business
Men's Fellowship International.

As this book goes to press, Jerome is celebrating his
eighty-seventh birthday.

HEALED, SAVED, SPIRIT-FILLED

"I'm so sorry to have to tell you this Jerome," said Dr. Pass. "We've done all we possibly can to help you, but both of your kidneys are totally destroyed. I estimate you have three more months at the most to live."

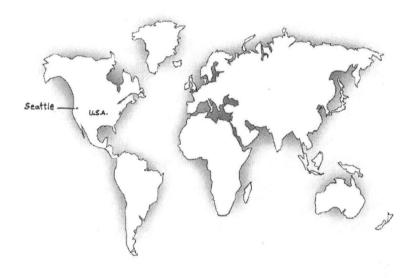

A death sentence! Jerome was devastated. At age thirty-seven he had a family to care for, and much more he wanted to do in his life. He had been struggling with excruciating pain from acute nephritis for seven years. Survival from a kidney transplant was slim in 1967, and he had been refused dialysis. The doctor's best advice: "Go home and get your affairs in order."

At first he was in denial. His world had completely collapsed. He began to sob, and the doctor sympathetically left him alone. He went home disappointed and discouraged, not knowing what to do. He hadn't told his wife, JoAnn, about the kidney machine, because he had wanted to surprise her with the wonderful news when he was accepted. Now that he had been denied, he couldn't bring himself to tell her all hope was gone.

He lay awake nights with the solitary burden, wondering how his family would make it without him. Finally he knew he had to tell JoAnn the truth. In great sorrow they straightened out their finances, bought grave lots, and prepared emotionally for his death.

Keith Gunn was an old friend of theirs from Wisconsin, and the only Christian they had ever known. He and his wife, Joanne, frequently told them they could be saved if they would accept Jesus Christ into their lives, and that Jerome could be healed through prayer. He had never heard of faith healing and wondered how prayer could help, but he wasn't desperate enough to call them.

A few months later he became worse--full of pain, his face and back a mass of sores. They had so many doctor bills he didn't want to go to the doctor, but finally JoAnn took him. The doctor said he had uremic poisoning, and needed to get to the hospital immediately. Four hours later they operated and removed his prostate gland.

Three days later, the night nurse discovered that his mattress and the floor were covered in blood. He passed out, and when he became conscious again, he saw people in white all around his bed, and heard JoAnn sobbing. He could hear doctors and nurses shouting orders as they frantically tried to save his life. He went unconscious again. Their voices faded.

Later when he came to, his sight was dim; the hospital room seemed very dark, and he could only see one man clearly – Keith Gunn.

Keith was standing over him, praying with one hand on his dying body, and the other raised in the air. Jerome could see doctors and nurses like shadows standing helplessly around the bed as his life's blood left him. Later Jerome recalled, "I distinctly felt as if I were sinking down into the mattress and would soon be gone. I was gripped by an unutterable fear of where I'd wake up tomorrow. I knew beyond a shadow of a doubt that I was lost and separated from God. If I could have found the strength, I would have screamed out in horror." As Keith continued to pray, he passed out again.

When he awoke in the morning, the nurse standing by his bed told him that sometime during the night the bleeding had completely stopped. He knew in his heart only God could have performed such a miracle. For the first time he knew God had touched his life, but he still wasn't ready to make Jesus his Lord and Master.

He remained in the hospital for a month before they were able to get him up and around. He was quite weak, but was finally able to leave and go back to work. After he used the bathroom at the plant, he left blood. Later someone came down and said, "Hey! Who's been bleeding? There is blood all over the urinal." He didn't say anything, because he needed the work badly, and didn't want them to send him home. Eventually he felt better, and he knew God was with him. He knew he shouldn't be alive. He knew he was in God's hands.

Around the same time, his oldest son, Jerry, was in despair. He was facing the draft and worrying about how the family would get along if his father were to die. He tried drugs, but they didn't bring any peace. In December he tried to commit suicide by taking a jumbo bottle of aspirins. The family didn't realize he had poisoned himself until the next morning.   As soon as they made that discovery, they rushed him to the hospital, but twenty minutes later the doctor told them it was too late-- there was no hope for him. The aspirins had already gone into his system, and it wasn't long before he went into convulsions.

For three days and nights he writhed and screamed in agony, tied down to the bed. Each time he came to, his face reflected the same tormenting fear that Jerome had felt. Jerry kept crying out, "I don't want to die now! I don't want to die!" During that time Jerome prayed in his own feeble way, "Oh God, if you will give my son back to me, I will serve you for the rest of my life."

Jerry began to show improvement, but the doctor said his mind would be destroyed because of his high fever and the condition of his blood.   But when he regained consciousness, he was completely normal! The doctors were astonished! They found out later that Keith Gunn and other members of his church had been praying constantly for him.   But still, Jerome wasn't ready to receive Jesus.

Finally in January 1968 the attack came they said would take his life.   His legs felt like they were twisted around backwards because the pain was so severe in his kidneys.   Then he remembered what Keith had said about being healed by prayer. He had nothing to lose, so he asked his wife to call the Gunns and ask them to come pray. Keith and Joanne came over and prayed for him that night. After praying for an hour, the pain in his back started to go away. They stayed and visited with them for a while, and by the time they left, Jerome had no more pain in his back. He was amazed!

They came to his house every night after that and prayed, and as they prayed, the sores began to heal. After three weeks, he had run out of his medicine, and he quit taking it. He felt so good that he missed his regular doctor's appointment. The nurse called to ask if he had passed away. "No," he said, "That's me talking!"

"Oh!" she said. "That's good! We've been keeping a bed reserved for you in the hospital because you were here so often, but right now we are filled to the limit, and I called to see if you could release the bed to somebody else."

"Sure," he said. "I'm feeling so good I don't need it anymore."

About five minutes later, Dr. Pass called. "What's this?" He asked. "You have no more pain?"

"No," he said. "And the sores I had all over my back and face have quit coming, and the old ones are healing up. I really feel good!"

"I want you in my office tomorrow morning," the doctor said. "I want you to come in for testing and x-rays."

Getting the x-rays the next day was a painful process, and Jerome was miserable. They took an x-ray, waited a while, and then took another. They took several. They took blood and urine tests. Finally the nurse told him to wait in the waiting room. He waited there a half hour until the nurse said, "The doctor wants to see you in his office."

The doctor sat at his desk staring at him, and then at the papers on his desk, but didn't say a word. Jerome sat down on a chair and waited, and finally the doctor shook his head and said, "I just don't understand it. In all the tests we took today, I can't see any sign of acute nephritis. Here, let me show you something."

He turned out the lights, and put a series of x-rays on the x-ray board. X-rays from two or three years previous showed both kidneys becoming increasing enlarged and blotchy with black spots. He took that one down and put up another one. That one showed scar tissue where the kidneys had been torn apart. Then he put up a third one, which showed the kidneys two to three times larger than normal, and they were completely black.

"Look at that," he said. "Your kidneys were only functioning at 15%. They had been destroyed by the disease. I don't understand how you could have been alive with kidneys like that. Now look at this. This is the one I took today," he said, and put up the latest x-ray. That one showed two perfect kidneys — perfect in size and color. There wasn't a spot on them. He couldn't believe what he saw. The doctor looked at them and looked at Jerome, then finally asked, "What did you do? What happened to you?"

Jerome then realized God had healed him. "I had a friend come and pray for me," he told him, "and God healed me."

The doctor replied, "No. I can't accept that. It's just

not right. That kind of thing just doesn't happen. It's not normal." He looked at the x-ray again and said, "I can't figure out what happened. Someone praying... I've never heard of such a thing in all my life. I'm going to have to think about this for a long time. I may have to accept the fact that God healed you, because there isn't any other way this could have happened." He stood up and shook Jerome's hand. "Keep on doing what you are doing", he said. "This is really wonderful."

When he went home that night, he called Joanne and Keith, and told them about the x-rays and what the doctor had said. They were thrilled, and asked, "Do you want to come to church with us?"

"Yes! I would." So they picked up Jerome and JoAnn and took them to church that night. It was a strange experience for them: people lifting their hands, swaying, with tears in their eyes, praising God. They spoke in languages he couldn't understand. Then he remembered Keith telling him that they were praying in a language God had given them. He said, "You don't understand, but their spirits are talking directly to God." He couldn't help but notice how happy the people were, and wished he could have what they had. He was in tears he wanted it so bad. He asked Keith, "Please pray for me. I want to have what they've got."

In those days the church met in the basement of Cal and Mary Freden's home in Seattle, Washington. Keith took him upstairs to one of the bedrooms to pray. They knelt down by a bed and Keith helped him receive Jesus Christ as his Lord and Savior. He knew beyond a doubt that Jesus lived, died and was raised from the dead. As Keith prayed, he encouraged

Jerome to keep praising God.

As Jerome tells it, "I began praising God and talking to Him. I had never done that before—it was so foreign to me. Then God began to fill me with His Spirit. All of a sudden I realized I was speaking in a different language. And I tell you, that's when I really felt the presence of God, His love, and peace. It was an experience I had never known was possible."

He didn't understand it--strange sounds, a foreign language, coming out of his mouth. He was overwhelmed with feelings of peace and joy, and he cried. Keith went downstairs and told JoAnn, Jerome was speaking in tongues. She came up because she didn't believe it, and had to see for herself. Soon she was beside him, accepting Jesus Christ, and receiving the Holy Spirit as well.

"Oh, I tell you," Jerome says, "life was so wonderful from then on! Our lives were so changed! What peace of mind I received when I finally met Jesus, the Lord of Glory, after so many years without Him. I found the truth in the scripture: 'He that heareth my word, and believeth on him that sent me, hath everlasting life, and shall not come into condemnation, but is passed from death unto life.' John 5:24. It was impossible for me to tell how much I loved Jesus."

The next day every time he closed his eyes, he started speaking in tongues. The following week he asked to be baptized by complete submersion, in the name of Jesus. Members of the church took Jerome and JoAnn to a lake, and baptized both of them. When he came up out of the water, he said, "Jesus Christ, all I have in this life I owe to you. Do with me whatever you want. Use me however you want, and I will do it for the rest of my life. I owe you that." He meant that with all his being. He knew God's promises for him—and it was so wonderful!

From then on, Jerome, JoAnn and their younger son, Joey, attended the church. Before long a church building was constructed, and they were excited about all that was happening.

Jerome had an urgency to pray for people. God had given him new kidneys, and he wanted everyone to experience what he had experienced—a tremendous healing. But his new faith was about to be severely tested.

One Sunday afternoon after church, he was working in the backyard, changing the oil in his '64 Plymouth. The car was quite low to the ground, so he lifted it with a hydraulic jack. Then he took a bumper jack and jacked it up higher so he could get under it. Lying on his side so oil wouldn't drip on him, he took three or four bolts out of it to drop the pan on the transmission. Suddenly, without warning, the car fell off the jack and fell on Jerome. The frame went across his chest, crushing it and the side of his face, pinning his head to the ground. He let out a scream with the little bit of air that was left in his lungs, and went totally numb. JoAnn heard his scream, ran out of the house, saw his condition, and tried in vain to work the jack. In desperation she came around the car and lifted that big, heavy Plymouth high enough for Jerome to get out from under it.

He stood up and saw his hideous looking chest caved in under his arm and bulged out in front. Completely numb and hardly able to breathe, he walked into the house with JoAnn's help, and lay on the davenport. It was difficult to lie down because his ribs were broken, but he managed to rest on his right side.

"Should I call an ambulance?" JoAnn asked. He shook his head, no. "Then what should I do, call the elders?" He nodded, yes. He must have passed out, because it seemed to him like three or four of the elders were there praying for him within minutes. One of them got right down by his mouth and said, "He's not breathing! He isn't taking in air! He's not breathing at all!" They laid their hands on him and began to pray fervently.

By this time his chest was one solid mass of unbearable pain, and he was going in and out of consciousness. He had been supporting himself on his right side with his elbow, but finally was so weak that he had to let himself lie on his back, on all those broken ribs. He heard a gurgling sound, the great bulge in the center of his chest fell down, and the pieces of his ribs fell into their normal places. The elders looked at him again, and one of them said, "He's breathing! I can feel a little breath now!"

Later Jerome said, "Deep down in my chest I could feel a tiny round spot about the size of a marble where there was no pain. This is the only way I can describe it. The elders continued to pray for me, and I felt the spot begin to spread. I thought that when it had filled my chest, I would be dead.

But I felt the spot slowly get bigger and bigger and finally the pain free area filled my whole chest. I couldn't feel any broken ribs, and the bulge went down to where it was supposed to be. Every time I tried to move a little bit, the pain was tremendous. So I lay very still. As long as I didn't move those ribs or take deep breaths, I had no pain. I couldn't believe it! God is so good!"

On Monday morning, JoAnn called his employer and told him Jerome had broken ribs, and wouldn't be in for work. He walked around the house to see what he could and couldn't do, and discovered that he could move around quite well without his ribs hurting much. Since they needed money, Wednesday night he decided to go to work on Thursday.

At his job as a journeyman diesel mechanic at the Metropolitan Bus Company, he repaired starters and alternators. Even though it hurt, he did his work that day as usual, picking up alternators from the floor and putting them on his bench so he could work on them. At the ten o'clock break, the foreman came up to him and said, "I've been watching you today, putting starters and alternators up on your bench. Three days ago your wife called and said you had broken ribs. You don't have broken ribs! She lied to me! Why were you off?"

Jerome opened his coveralls, took the foreman's hand, put it on his side, pushed in, and the ribs buckled underneath his hand. The foreman pulled his hand out, turned absolutely white, turned and walked off. He had great respect for Jerome after that--- knowing that he was working in spite of broken ribs.

Jerome went to church Friday evening scared, because he knew he would have to tell about what had happened. He had never spoken before a crowd, and sure enough the pastor asked him to give his testimony because everybody in the church had prayed for him. He walked to the front, knees shaking because he was afraid to speak to all those people. He didn't even know what to say!

He looked at the people, then started speaking. All fear left as he told about the car falling on him, crushing his chest and breaking his ribs. He told about the elders coming and praying, and how God had healed him. He suddenly realized he wasn't thinking those things! The Lord was speaking through him as he listened to his own voice. Then he heard himself ask all who were sick to come forward to be healed.

That was something he had never done before. He was so nervous he didn't even remember what he prayed. As he prayed for them one by one, they were all healed. When he went back to his pew, he leaned back into his seat, but there wasn't any pain! He felt under his arm and on his backbone. He twisted around and put his hand on his ribs and pushed, discovering that they were completely solid. When he first got up to speak, he could feel his ribs grinding together as he moved. But while he was praying for others, God finished healing him as well!

After the service he asked a couple of elders to push on his ribs, to see if they were still broken. They pushed and pushed, but Jerome didn't feel any pain. God had healed his ribs under his arm, and where they attached to his back! He even pounded on them to demonstrate the fact. That was the first time he experienced God healing bones. What a thrill!

He could hardly wait to get home to pray, and he prayed all night long, thanking and praising God for the healing He had given. He was so excited he had to tell everybody what he had experienced. It was a tremendous time in his life. God showed Jerome He could heal kidneys, and now He had healed bones as well. Jerome went everywhere telling people what

God had done, and prayed for them. He knew it wasn't just for him — it was for everybody.

For certain, only God could do this!

GOD'S CALL

"Look at your hands," an audible voice said. It startled Jerome. He looked around but saw no one, then asked, "What was that?" He thought there was something wrong with his hands, so he looked at them. Then the voice said, "Those hands are my hands. Place them on my people, and they will be healed."

After he came to the Lord, Jerome spent many hours alone up in the mountains seeking God and His will for his life. He wanted to serve his Lord, Jesus, but didn't know how. He hung a piece of plastic over a rope that he tied between two trees, with a sleeping bag under it. Then he built a little fire next to it, which he kept feeding, and prayed all night long. As he prayed he felt the strong presence of God. He loved it so much that he went there at every opportunity.

On one of those occasions he was sitting on a stump by the fire, looking up, praising God. It was then that he heard God's voice, promising to heal the sick through his hands. He thought he might be imagining things, since the emotion of his healing was so intense. He wanted everyone to be healed just as God had healed him. But the message made sense, and he was overjoyed. He told JoAnn about it, but asked her not to tell anyone about it yet, because he wanted to be sure it was from God.

Another time it was as though God wasn't there. He tried to pray, but didn't feel God's presence. He felt disappointed, so he packed up and went back down the mountain. When he got to his car, he sat on a big rock and rested. Then he heard, "I'm up here."

He thought he was hearing things, but then he heard it again, "I'm up here. Look up here."

He looked up and as he did he could feel himself lifting off the rock-- up and up above the tree tops. In front of him was a crowd of people, and he felt a hand on his right shoulder. As he looked at the crowd, he could see that it was in a large outdoor meeting. In front was a man on a platform, but he was too far away for Jerome to identify. Then a hand waved, and he felt himself going down into the back of the crowd.

The man on the platform was praying for people. Some were going off in one direction, and some the other way. As he looked at them, he noticed that the people in one group were cripples, bent over, with canes or in wheel chairs. After they were prayed for they walked and danced, cried and shouted. The ones that went the other way were also praising God as they went.

He wanted to see what was going on, so he started working his way through the crowd He had a hard time getting through because there were so many people, but finally he was able to see the man on the platform. He was so startled he could only stare. The man on the platform was himself. He then knew this was what God wanted him to do.

He looked back, and when he did, the crowd was gone, and he was sitting on the big rock. It was a vision from God. He sat there for two or three hours, thinking about it and remembering what he had seen. He wondered how there could be so many people in an open field. What would draw them, and how could it take place?

He was afraid to tell anyone about the vision, afraid they would think he was full of pride, and that he had dreamed it. But he knew it wasn't a dream--it was too real. So he only told JoAnn about it. Much later when he was ministering in Africa, he frequently led outdoor meetings — there was no other place. He then remembered that vision.

One spring there was still some snow on the ground. He lay under his tarp, praising God and rejoicing in His presence. Oh how he loved that! Then suddenly he heard footsteps near him. He sat up and looked around the plastic, and there was a bear about four feet away. The only thing he had for protection was his hunting knife, so he quietly got on the other side of the fire and built it up. Each time the bear came from one direction, he'd go to the opposite side of the fire. He was really frightened, so he did that all night long, knowing that the bear wouldn't attack that close to a fire.

Finally the bear went away, and Jerome praised God for His protection. When morning came, he packed his stuff in a hurry and quickly hiked out. Bears aren't normally aggressive, but he thought it might have been a sow with her cub, and he didn't want to take any chances.

It was a month before he could go to the mountains again, but he didn't want to go near that place. He found a different location, where he could commune with the Lord, even in the winter, in the snow. What wonderful times he had with the Lord up in the mountains.

For a while he wondered if people believed his healing testimony. He felt he had to prove his experiences were true and real. But God spoke to his heart: "That's not your problem. That's their problem. Don't worry about it anymore. Just keep telling people what I have done, and if they don't believe you that will be their problem, not yours. " What a relief! All Jerome had to do was tell the truth, and he didn't have to prove anything. From then on it was easy for him to share his testimony.

Jerome's experiences were unique. God allowed him to go through those things for a testimony — so people could see how God works, time after time — mending bones, giving new kidneys, healing whatever was needed, and then believing Him-- believing in His power, His love, and His promises.

As Jerome would say, "'Ask anything in my name and I will do it', God says. That is no lie. God put that in the scriptures. We need to grab hold of those scriptures to know that they are for each and every one of us. Whenever we have troubles we have the book of life — written by God for every one of us, whether we are injured or sick or whatever.

He has put in His book that if we will call upon His name He will heal us. It's up to each of us to believe it. Jesus Christ took stripes upon His back for us, and it's already written in the book of life. All you have to do is accept it. Ask for it in the name of Jesus Christ, and know that His promises are still true for us.

I have experienced it over and over again in my life. I owe God my very life. The things I have gone through seem preposterous, and yet God allowed me to go through them, so I could tell people that He has deliverance for every one of us. Just reach out to God and say, 'Deliver me, Lord.' Put your eyes upon Jesus Christ, not upon the circumstances, and He will deliver and heal you. 'By His stripes we are healed.'"

Yes, it's true. . .Only God could do this.

THE BEGINNING OF THE MINISTRY

"What are you doing? You can't go in there! You might spread germs from person to person!" said a nurse in the hospital Jerome was visiting.

After he was healed, saved and Spirit-filled, he had an urgency to pray for people—for God to heal others as He had healed him. He visited the sick in their homes and in hospitals, and offered to pray for them.

Since he wasn't allowed to enter hospital rooms of strangers, he watched, and when the nurses weren't looking, he'd sneak into a room. When a patient didn't want to be prayed for, he went to another room. He had such satisfaction in bringing hope and the presence of God to them, it didn't bother him if he didn't see them healed instantly.

The elders of the church visited the sick of the congregation, and sometimes Jerome went with them. After a month or so, they began to see instant healings as they prayed. What a joy! After a while the elders came to Jerome and said that the only times they saw miracle healings was when he was with them. That was hard for him to believe, but when they told him about the healings they had seen, he began to realize that God was using him. He kept going wherever he could to pray for people, and they were healed consistently.

At church he asked the pastor if he could pray for people after services, and with his permission he did. People lined up, and he prayed for them. After a while as he looked at the people waiting, he knew their problems. He was troubled because he didn't know if God was giving him that knowledge, or if it was from his own mind. So before the next service, he wrote a list of ten prayer needs for that night that came to him as he was praying. He gave the list to one of the elders and said, "These are the needs that will be prayed for tonight."

He watched as they came for prayer, and found their problems on the list. However there was one that didn't come — a person with nose bleeds. But later one little boy said, "There was a guy in the bathroom with a terrible nose bleed!" That was confirmation that indeed God was showing him needs ahead of time. God had given him the gifts of healing and of the word of knowledge, as are mentioned in the Bible.

Another night Jerome asked the pastor if he could do things a little differently. The pastor said he was doing well, and gave him permission. That night during the service, as he looked out at the congregation, his eyes stopped on one person, and God revealed his problem to him. He described the problem and said, "I want you to come up." When the person came up and verified it, Jerome prayed for him and he was healed. Then when Jerome looked around at others, God revealed their problems, he called them to the front, and God healed them also.

He attended chapter meetings of the Full Gospel Business Men's Fellowship International (FGBMFI), hoping to pray for people. His reputation proceeded him, so people were eager to receive prayer. Even though he had never seen those people before, and didn't know anything about them, God revealed their problems to him. After Jerome called them forward, they verified their needs, he prayed for them, and they were healed. Soon he got invitations to minister in other chapters.

Then his ministry went beyond Seattle. Keith Gunn had moved back to Eau Claire, Wisconsin, where he pastored a church. Jerome and JoAnn went there on vacation, and ministered in his church, and then to other churches in the area. God moved in wonderful ways, and Jerome was kept quite busy. When pastors heard about his ministry, they asked him to return, which he did quite often.

While in Wisconsin they always visited his parents. His father asked him many questions, and finally asked, "Do you suppose Jesus would come and save me?"

"Of course!" Jerome answered, and he accepted Christ that day.

On another occasion he did a service near Grantsburg, his home town, and his parents attended. At the close of the service, Jerome asked if anyone wanted to give his life to the Lord. His mother cautiously put up her hand, but then put it down again. Jerome was so full of joy he couldn't say anything. Then she raised her hand again, looked at him and waved. She came to the front of the church, and Jerome had the privilege of ushering his own mother into God's kingdom. What a wonderful blessing for him to help bring both of his parents to salvation!

At that time he was working for the Metropolitan Bus Company as a diesel mechanic. His ministry was growing, and fortunately his boss was wonderful about letting him take time off for ministry.

The Full Gospel Businessmen's Fellowship has short-term missionary trips to other countries, which they call "airlifts". In 1972 Jerome and several other men went on one, they paid all their own expenses. JoAnn didn't go with them that time, because it was only for men.

They first went to London, England, where they attended a Billy Graham Crusade. Demos Shakarian, the founder and head of the Full Gospel Businessmen's Fellowship, talked to Billy Graham before the service. After a while the two of them came over to a group of them, and Billy said, "Jerome?"

"Yes, that's me", Jerome said. Then Billy shook his hand.

"I've heard good things about you. I want you to sit on the platform while I preach tonight." Jerome felt excited and honored to do so. Afterwards he wanted to talk to Billy again, but there were so many people around him that he didn't get the opportunity.

After London they went to Brussels, where they had three meetings, and from there twenty of them went to Johannesburg, South Africa. Demos set up groups to go to various places. When he asked, "Who wants to minister in the black section?" not one person raised his hand. So Jerome raised his hand and said, 'I will, I will!'

When he went, the Lord worked many miracles. The black people were most grateful that he would come to minister to them, and many attended the meeting. The second night, the street was filled with people walking to the church. When he got there, the church was already filled. The windows and double doors were opened so people standing outside could hear.

Jerome didn't prepare his messages ahead of time, because he wanted the Lord to be in control. The Holy Spirit reminded him of certain Bible passages or testimonies, and the messages were never the same. God then gave him the word of knowledge for the people, and Jerome prayed for them. At first he stood on a platform, but soon there were so many people that had come forward, he couldn't stay there — he had to go down to them.

Once as he was reading from the Bible, an usher came and whispered to him that there was a man passed out on the sidewalk. Jerome said, "There is an emergency. I'll be right back."

He went as quickly as he could, but the man appeared dead. He put his hand on the man's forehead and prayed for him. He opened his eyes, looked at Jerome, and then at the people around him. "How are you feeling?" Jerome asked.

"I think I'm going to be all right now," he answered. Jerome helped him up and into the building, sat him in the front row, then went back to the platform to continue speaking. Many people gave their hearts to the Lord that night. The people were so hungry for the word of God that they had six more packed out meetings that week.

The man that had appeared dead attended all the meetings. Before the last meeting Jerome saw the man sitting in the front row, went over to him and asked, "How are you feeling?"

"Oh I'm perfect," he said. "I had a heart disease, and I wasn't able to get out of bed for a long time. But when I heard about you being here, I just had to come. I came and got as far as the door, and then collapsed. But since that day I have never had trouble with my heart. It's all fine." God is so good!

On Wednesday night, all the groups got together, and had a service with the people from the airlift. Demos spoke first about what the Full Gospel Business Men's Fellowship was doing in that area, and then gave testimonies of what the other men had done. Then he called Jerome. "Take as long as you want," he said.

As Jerome was giving his testimony, a woman in the front row started shaking violently, fell out of her chair, and onto the floor. He went down and held her face with a hand on each cheek to hold her still. He looked at her and prayed, then all of a sudden she became quiet. When he asked, "What happened?" her husband said, "She had another epileptic seizure." He had someone get her a large cup of water, and she sipped on that while he finished ministering.

He didn't want to make his ministry seem more effective than the others', so he didn't say much about the healings that occurred. But he didn't have to. They had all heard about them.

The following night, the black Christians wanted to have a big banquet in his honor. What wonderful food they had! They insisted that Jerome go through the food line first. He felt embarrassed, but did anyway. As they were eating, some of the other men from the airlift came, but the black Christians wouldn't allow them to eat with them. The blacks didn't want to mix with the whites, so Jerome was the only white person there. It was such an honor!

They had the next night off, and the next day they were to return to London. The couple with the epileptic wife came to the hotel to see Jerome, and they told him that since he prayed for her, she hadn't had another seizure. Before then, she had had several a day. They asked Jerome to come to their small furniture store the next day and minister to their employees. They set up benches in the loading dock, and made a platform for him to stand on. After his testimony, Jerome asked if any wanted to know this Jesus Christ that he knows, and if so to stand up. They all stood up! He told them to come forward, and then he jumped down off the platform and asked them to repeat: "Lord Jesus Christ. . .I want You to receive me as your child. . . Forgive me of my sins, . . .that I might know You. . . . I believe that you died on a cross, and rose again. . . . Amen."

Everyone spoke the prayer after him, all the way through. He jumped back up on the platform, and the man and his wife came and thanked him over and over. The man said, "From now on I'm going to have someone come here and minister to these people just as you did now. And I'm going to pay their wages while they are listening. That was a real blessing."

After they flew back to London, they had four days for sightseeing before returning to the United States, but Jerome and Peter Congelier wanted to minister instead. They talked to Demos, who said, "There was another meeting planned in Sweden, but the guys are pretty tired, so I cancelled it."

Peter said, "May Jerome and I go?"

"Sure. Go ahead," Demos said. He gave them the name of the Swedish pastor, and off they went — first by plane to Copenhagen, then by boat to southern Sweden.

They didn't know the name of the church, so it was a while before they were able to find the pastor. When they finally did, he said, "We thought the meeting was cancelled, so we don't have one planned for tonight. But I'll tell you what. Since you're here I'll call around and see if we can get some here for a meeting." He did, about 30 people came, and it was a great blessing. The pastor took Jerome's name and number, and hoped that he would come again.

The next day they went back to London, and then returned home with the Full Gospel Businessmen. That was Jerome's first airlift, and that was just the beginning.

Truly only God could do this.

IRELAND AND ENGLAND

"May I pray for you?" The man asked. Could a minister of healing be healed when prayed for by a brand new Christian? Jerome came to England to pray for the sick, but here was a man in a wheelchair offering to pray for *him*. He pondered that question for just a moment, then humbly submitted.

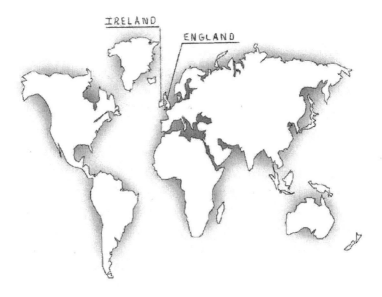

On August 30th Jerome and JoAnn went to Belfast, Ireland. There they were met by Allen Cunningham, and taken to a farm on a hill overlooking the city of Belfast. Walter and Anne Galloway, owners of the farm, were excellent hosts and they stayed with them for two and a half weeks. During that time they ministered in many church services and F.G.B.M.F.I. chapter meetings.

One of those meetings was attended by a woman in a wheelchair. Jerome wheeled her to the front and asked her about her problem. She told him she had a stroke the previous year, and her left arm and left leg were paralyzed. He asked her to show him if she could walk. She said, "If you will help me up, I will try."

He lifted her out of the wheelchair, and saw that her left leg was completely useless. He set her down on a chair, and prayed for her. Lifting her off of the chair, he said, "Let's see if the Lord has healed you."

With the first step she took, her leg supported her weight and with each step it got stronger. On the fifth step Jerome pulled away from her, and she grabbed for his hand. She held his index finger as they walked up and down the aisle of the church. Her husband jumped to his feet and shouted, "SHE CAN'T DO THAT!" as he watched her walk up and down the aisle with her leg that was no longer paralyzed.

In an F.G.B.M.F.I. meeting, a man brought his son, and they sat near the back of the room. God revealed to Jerome that the son had a stomach problem. He went to the boy and told him that he had bleeding in his stomach. The boy said that was true. Jerome prayed for him and told him that he had been healed, and there would be no more bleeding. After the meeting, his father told Jerome that the doctor said disease had totally destroyed the boy's stomach. He was scheduled to have surgery in one week to take out his stomach and most of his intestines, and put in a colostomy bag.

Ten days later at another meeting, they came again. The boy asked if he could give a testimony. He told the people that when Jerome prayed for him, Jesus healed him, and the bleeding completely stopped. The following day he felt so much better, he worked in the yard. Each day he was able to do more work around the yard. When he went back to the doctor, he had gained seven pounds in seven days, and he was told that he didn't need surgery. The doctor told him that whatever he was doing to just keep doing it.

Many more miracles and healings took place on that trip, but the greatest miracle happened in England, while staying in the home of Rodney Radcliffe. Jerome and JoAnn went for a walk one afternoon, and she went into one shop while he was headed for another. On the way, he came to a place where the sidewalk dropped about four inches. He didn't see it, stumbled and fell. He had packages in each hand, so he put his arm across his chest to cushion his fall. Unfortunately he hit the edge of the curb with the center of his arm, breaking the bone. He lay there in tremendous pain. People in the store came out and helped him to his feet. He had a small cut on his hand so they took him into the store, wiped the blood off his hand and applied a Band-Aid.

They felt his arm, told him it was broken and asked if they could call an ambulance. Jerome refused, saying that he would be fine, and that he just had a block to go. The pain was unbearable, but he was able to find his wife in the store where he had left her, and they immediately returned to Rodney's house. After they got there, Jerome told them what had happened. Rodney's wife, a nursing instructor in a college in London, examined his arm, said indeed it was broken, and said he should get it plastered (have a cast put on it). They all prayed for Jerome, but he received no relief from the pain.

He felt a cast on his arm wouldn't inspire faith in the people, so he talked to the Lord about it. "Lord,

I'm going to finish the twelve meetings I have left with a broken arm, unless You heal me."

He determined not to let the devil get the victory and stop him. His arm was so painful he couldn't do anything for himself, so JoAnn had to dress him. At the meeting that night, the pain was so bad he couldn't keep his mind on what he was saying. After he repeated himself several times, he stopped speaking.

He wanted to explain why he was having so much trouble keeping his mind on what he was saying, so he pulled up his sleeve, and when he gripped his hand tight, the bone in his arm bulged out. Several people came up, felt his arm and felt the separation of the bone. There were about fifty people there that night, and they all saw that his arm was broken.

Jerome couldn't go on, so he cut the service short. He asked for those that wanted to give their hearts to the Lord to come forward. Four people came up and accepted the Lord. One was a man in a wheelchair. He told him that he broke his back just below his neck twenty-two years earlier, and he had been paralyzed ever since. Jerome prayed for him, and as soon as he finished, the man wanted to pray for Jerome. As he prayed, he held Jerome's arm tightly, and he could feel the bone buckle. The more he squeezed, the less pain Jerome felt, so Jerome began to examine his arm. He had no pain, and the bone would not give when he pressed on it. He began to pound on his arm where the bone had been broken, and still there was no pain. Watching that made JoAnn sick to her stomach. Many others turned pale and turned away, not believing that God could instantly heal a broken bone.

But the man in the wheelchair said, "Now I believe! Now I believe!" He lifted himself up with his hands and began to move his hips from side to side and back and forth, showing he had movement in his hips. He couldn't move his legs yet, but he knew that would come. When he saw God heal Jerome's broken arm, he believed for his own healing. He accepted the Lord just before he prayed for Jerome, daring to believe the Word of God and His promises. The congregation greatly rejoiced knowing that God answers everyone's prayers.

After Jerome and JoAnn came back to the United States, they received several reports of healings God had performed because of his ministry. He was as blessed as the people to whom he had ministered, knowing that only God could do this.

SWEDEN, FINLAND, LENINGRAD

"They weren't supposed to advertise! Let's get out of here!" Jerome's alarmed host said, as they looked at notices with Jerome's picture posted everywhere. They were in Leningrad, behind the iron curtain, and Jerome's ministry to a small group of people was supposed to be a secret meeting.

At first Jerome was afraid, and wanted to follow his advice, but he prayed, and the Lord filled him with peace. "Let's go anyway and see what God will do."

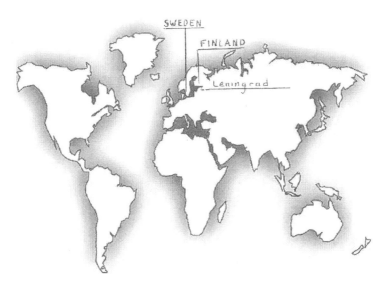

Jerome travelled and ministered in Sweden seven times. He spoke Swedish, so he didn't need a translator. After his first airlift in 1972, ministers from Sweden contacted him, and asked him to come back. He took one more trip with the full Gospel Businessmen's Fellowship in 1996, and five other trips with JoAnn. On one of those trips he also went to Finland and Leningrad, Russia.

Once he went to the People's Church for a crusade where they met every day for two weeks. Jerome went to a couple of meetings, but there wasn't anything for him to do, so he asked the pastor's advice. "Would you like to go to our sister church in Finland?" he asked.

"Sure, "Jerome said, "That would be good." So he travelled by ship to Helsinki. The next day, several people were waiting for him at the dock, and they took him to a hotel. That night they had a service in their church, a huge dome carved out of a mountain. The beautiful building could hold up to six hundred people, and the acoustics were outstanding. People in the back of the sanctuary could hear the speaker clearly without the aid of a microphone.

Their band was on one side, and they played many lovely songs that were unfamiliar to Jerome. Then he gave his testimony, adding appropriate scriptures he had memorized. They knew those scriptures well, but what they needed was healing, so Jerome prayed for them. The next night he spoke less and prayed more, because that was why they came. The third night he didn't speak at all—He just prayed for people, and many were healed.

The following day he went farther north to a Swedish section of Finland. When he arrived, people were looking for him. He had been asked to wear a carnation in his lapel, and they found him right away. They had small services for around thirty people, which made it possible for Jerome to minister to each person individually. God told Jerome something about each one of them, and they knew it was the word of the Lord for them. It raised their faith, and many were healed.

Later he went to a Finnish church. He didn't know Finnish, so didn't speak much. He prayed for them and exercised the gift of knowledge.

He kept going north, and on the first of September, arrived in a town with four feet of snow. Because of the cold, brick or cement houses had walls three feet thick, and only three windows. The man he visited had a factory that made wood furniture. He had small rooms for his employees, where they could stay overnight if it was too cold for them to go home. A big boiler in a separate building burned sawdust from the mill for heat. A conveyor belt moved green sawdust over the top of the furnace and dried it. It then dropped sawdust into the fire. The boiler heated water in pipes, then hot water was piped into the building to warm it. Jerome thought it was a beautiful set-up.

Wood was hard to get. In Finland and Sweden every tree was registered, and marked with a serial number. People had to have permission to cut a tree, and have a plan for all parts of it, including the limbs. There was absolutely no waste. At the factory, they cut the grain of the wood, then intertwined light and dark grains to make beautiful furniture. Jerome ministered in the warm factory, because it cost too much to heat a meeting hall. There were about twenty people there, and they had three services.

He then spent two nights on a train travelling back to Helsinki. Each train car was small, with four partitions that contained a davenport, two bunks, a table, and a window on one side. If a person jumped up and down, everyone could feel the whole car wiggle. Four cars of people met Jerome, and they took him back to the church deep in the rock.

His plane was leaving soon, but they said they would get him back in time to catch it. Another American was speaking there, but they took him off the platform, because they wanted to hear Jerome. He talked about the meetings he had in Finland, then one of the men closed the service and got him to the airport on time.

On a different trip to Sweden, a lady called Jerome, concerned about her sister. She had been taking care of her sister for a long time, and wanted him to pray for her. He felt impressed by the Lord that she should be in a wheelchair when he arrived. The lady didn't think that was possible, because her sister had been bedridden for three months with a bad case of vertigo. But Jerome encouraged her to do all they could to get her in a wheelchair before he came.

When he arrived, he saw three women sitting at a table on a patio, and one was in a wheelchair. He introduced himself, started talking with them, and asked the sister about her condition. "When you can't walk," she said, "it's not worth living. I don't want to go on like this. I've given up on life."

They had tea and crumpets, then he walked behind her, put his hands on her shoulders and prayed, "Lord Jesus, encourage her to get up and walk right now. Let her know that this is the day You will do something for her. We ask these things in Your name."

Then he walked in front of her, stood four feet from her and said, "Stand up!"

She gave him a strange look and squirmed. Finally she said, "Ok, I'll try."

She then surprised herself by standing up. She wasn't dizzy, and wasn't holding on to anything.

"Come to me," Jerome said.

She stepped toward him, and he stepped back. "Now see what God has done. He has healed you. You can do whatever you want. God has healed you."

They walked around while her brother followed her with the wheelchair. He was concerned that she would fall. He *knew* she would fall, but she never did. She laughed and laughed. They walked around, had more tea, and visited some more. God showed them all a miracle — of someone healed of vertigo.

On a trip to Malmo, Sweden, Jerome was asked if he and his wife would go to a dairy farm east of the city. The farmer and his wife had a little girl with no tear ducts. They had to put drops in her eyes many times a day, and they asked Jerome to pray for her. He put his fingers over her eye lids and prayed. "Lord there is something wrong here, and I'm asking you to repair it. Make her eyes normal, and allow tears to come. Show them a miracle today."

As he prayed he felt moisture under his fingers. He pulled away and there were tears coming down her face. When her parents saw it, they cried, and Jerome cried with them. The little girl cried for three hours before the tears stopped.

Jerome travelled all through Sweden, city after city. There was tremendous excitement concerning his visits, but he couldn't get to all the places that wanted him — there were just too many. One was a big church of two thousand people. He wasn't scheduled to be there, but they replaced the scheduled speaker with Jerome. He wanted the other speaker to be included, so after he preached, he asked him to pray with him for people to accept Christ.

Gothenburg is a beautiful city on the west coast of Sweden. Canals enable big barges to go to all the parts of the city. Once he got to ride on one. The bridges were only six feet above the water, so Jerome, being over six feet tall, had to sit down when they went under them.

For thirty-seven days Jerome and JoAnn stayed in a castle in Gothenburg. Built in 1636, it was five stories high, and had walls four feet thick. Even though they were the only guests there, it was completely staffed. Their hosts provided a chauffeured limo for them, butlers and cooks. They got to stay in that castle every time they went to Sweden. They rode in the limo northwest of Stockholm, way up in the mountains. There were twenty beautiful acres of flat land with a nursing home, hotel and resort on top of a mountain. They stayed there, enjoyed the views and tame deer that came very close to them.

Every time he went to Sweden, he ministered in Stockholm in a Pentecostal church of two thousand people. But he didn't have the same opportunity in the Lutheran churches, where pastors were hired by the government. Most of those churches were afraid to have Jerome speak, for fear he would say something against their religion. But one church invited him. The Pastor was required to be there to open the meeting and pray over the service, but then he would leave. So Jerome was free to say what he wanted, and prayed for them. After the people saw healings, a big percentage were saved.

One of the men had a large lump on the side of his head. The doctor had removed the right side of his skull to give the brain tumor room to grow. When Jerome asked him questions, he could only give simple answers, and he couldn't say his own name. Jerome prayed for him, but didn't see any evidence of healing. He was disappointed, because it would have been a great testimony to the others.

A year later, he went to the church again. As he talked to some people at the front of the building before the service started, a man suddenly began yelling from the back of the church. He ran to Jerome, picked him up and whirled him around and around. Jerome was shocked. "Don't you don't know who I am?" the man asked.

"No," Jerome replied.

"I'm the guy with the bulge on the side of my head. I had a brain tumor. After you prayed, it started going down, and finally went away. I didn't have an operation or anything, and I can talk perfectly!" The doctor had to place a metal cap on his head to cover the place where part of his skull had been removed. He rapped on the metal, to show Jerome where it was.

That man's testimony was well known, so when Jerome got there the place was full. What a great day that was! All were healed. He didn't get a chance to testify because people came up right away, and asked for prayer. They all knew that man and had seen the results of his miracle from the Lord. God was there long before Jerome arrived. It was a tremendous healing service — the most spiritual service in which he had ever participated.

Once during an evening service, as he was up in front in a small church, he felt someone behind him. "Who is that?" he wondered. He turned around to look, but there was only an empty chair. Then he felt a hand on his right shoulder, as if someone was right beside him, but there was no one else on the platform. He concluded, "This has got to be the Lord." He was excited to think that God would support him so tangibly.

All of a sudden there was day light all around. He continued to minister, with that presence beside him. It was something he had never experienced before or since. It felt like an angel, perhaps six inches taller than he, standing alongside him. The Lord spoke through Jerome. He didn't even have to think about what he was preaching. After the service people asked, "What was that light all about?" Jerome didn't know. He could only suspect.

Later, one of the men told him that he had walked out of the building to check on his dog, and he could see daylight everywhere. A few days later it was reported in the newspaper--the whole town was lit up, and nearly everyone in the town saw it. No one could understand what caused it, but the presence of God was overwhelming.

Another time in Finland, Jerome went north to the Russian border, where they had a meeting set up for him in Leningrad. (Leningrad is now called St. Petersburg, its name before the formation of the Soviet Union.) His host told him he often shopped in Russia, so he could get Jerome over the border behind the iron curtain. When they got to the border, the guard knew the man, and waved them on. When they got to Leningrad, there were posters with Jerome's picture everywhere. His host said, "They weren't supposed to advertise! Let's get out of here!"

At first Jerome was afraid, and wanted to follow his advice, but he prayed, and the Lord filled him with peace. "Let's go anyway and see what God will do."

They went to a meeting upstairs in a restaurant at ten o'clock in the morning. Jerome began speaking, with his host translating for him. Jerome asked if any of them wanted to accept Jesus Christ, but no one dared to, because it could mean imprisonment. "Say these words after me, and you can be saved later if you wish," said Jerome. "Just say, 'Jesus, please forgive my sins and come into my heart. Come be the Master of my life.'" Laying their fears aside, they all repeated his words.

Jerome tried to close the service at noon, but no one left; so he preached some more, and shared what the Lord had done for him. Then he said, "If you have a physical problem, raise your hand." Many of them did, and Jerome prayed for them. At one-thirty he tried to close the meeting again, but still no one would go. He needed to leave, so he shook hands with the people and blessed them as he worked his way out the door. No one broke up the meeting, or bothered him the entire trip.

Two months later, the Finnish host called Jerome back in Seattle. He said he was shopping in Leningrad, when a man approached him and said, "I was in the KGB and was assigned to your meeting, but I was so interested in what the speaker was saying, I didn't break it up, as I was supposed to. I just let it go, because it was a blessing to me, and I want to become a Christian."

Yes, Jerome stepped out in faith in the Lord Jesus, who led and protected him, and proved again that only God could do this.

INDIA

"Will you come to India?" That question was asked Jerome while at a convention of the Full Gospel Businessmen's Fellowship International in Nashville, Tennessee in 1997.

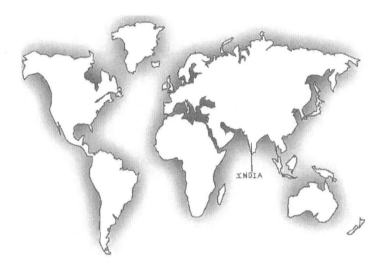

JoAnn and Jerome were outside their hotel room overlooking the balcony, when a man approached them. "My name is Ernest Komanapalli, of Manna Ministries," he said. "I have a big church, hospital and orphanage in India, and I would like you to come minister there. I have smaller contacts in other cities as well. We could keep you busy for a while." Jerome wasn't sure the Lord wanted him to go to India, but they exchanged phone numbers, just in case.

The following year Jerome felt the Lord's leading, so in 1998, He called Ernest and said he could come for two weeks. A couple months before he was to leave, Rev. David Jones of New Life Bible Fellowship, a man he had met at a Full Gospel Businessmen's meeting in Seattle, called and wanted to go. Jerome was glad for the company, because JoAnn didn't want to go to a third world country, thinking it was too dangerous. David agreed to pay his own way, because Jerome didn't want to charge a third world country for his ministry, since the people there are so poor. David's church gave him the money to go, and they went in March 1998.

They flew to London, then to Brussels, and then to Bombay, India. England ruled India for many years, and the English changed the name of the city to Bombay. After the English liberated India, the name was changed back to Mumbai, in honor of their Hindu goddess, Mumbadadevi. While waiting at the airport, they saw six little children begging for food. Jerome didn't pay any attention to them, but David couldn't stand it, and gave them each a dollar bill. The children ran to a lady sitting against a wall, and gave her the money. Then they came running back and held onto David's legs. He had a terrible time getting free.

Dr. Ernest Komanapalli picked up Jerome and David, and took them to Hyderabad, which means "bad water". That was a good name for it. The water tasted terrible. He owned a hotel, a hospital for twenty-six people, and a large orphanage for about one hundred fifty children. They had school for the children, all the way up through high school. Then the young people went to Trade school for two years, where they could learn to earn a living. Ernest was a real blessing to orphans there.

As they walked through town to the orphanage, they were shocked at conditions. The people were extremely poor, in bondage to Hinduism and Islam, with no hope for change. As they walked by, they saw children sitting on a wall. Many of them had birth defects as a result of interbreeding. One boy's feet were backwards. There was a well twelve feet across, with rock all around the edge, and stairs going down into it. People had to go down to the very bottom to get water for the orphanage.

In the orphanage there was a bunk house for the small children with no windows, and the smell of urine about knocked Jerome over. The children had to sleep there every night in awful conditions. Older children did the cleaning, but didn't have enough time to get things really clean. There were four bunks on each wall, and a double row of bunks through the middle of the room. It was a different world than they had ever seen. Only God knew how Ernest could buy food for all of the children. His dedication was admirable. He was truly a man of God as he gave his life for those children.

Jerome and David were there fourteen days, and they ministered every day. Jerome taught in the Bible College for an hour each morning. Several afternoons David and Jerome ministered in hospitals and orphanages, and one leper colony. Each evening they ministered in churches, from Hyderabad to the east coast of India. Travel was by train, taxi, three-wheel jitney, and walking, walking, walking.

Ernest had a friend in the hospital and asked, "Will you go and pray for my friend? She has heart trouble, and is going to have open heart surgery in a couple of days." She already had shunts in her wrist, in preparation for the surgery. They went to the hospital and Jerome talked to her but there was no response. As he laid his hands on her and prayed, she opened her eyes, saw Ernest, and began to speak. Jerome prayed some more, and the Lord took all the pain from her chest. As they were talking, she sat on the edge of the bed, then got up and walked around the room. Then she asked, "Will you pray for my friends?" So they prayed for her friends in the hospital. They prayed for everyone in the hospital. Ernest was amazed at how well she was. Jesus had instantly healed her. Doctors kept her in the hospital for two more days, trying to understand what had happened. Finally they discharged her without surgery.

One evening they had a street meeting. There were houses built on a long wall on the street, with doors going into each home. Ernest made a three foot high platform out of shipping crates, and had one lightbulb shining over Jerome. People filled the street as far as he could see in both directions, and they squatted in front of him to listen. When he began speaking, a little white goat jumped onto the platform, pushed up against his leg, and fell asleep at his feet.

It was so crowded, Jerome could only pray for them as a group. He gave his testimony and a salvation message. He asked them to stand, and all of them stood. Then he said, "Repeat after me: Lord Jesus Christ,. . . come into my heart,. . . forgive me of my sins. . . take me as Your child. . . .Amen." As soon as he said "Amen", the little goat got up, jumped off the platform and left.

One of the men came up and said to the crowd, "If you want, you may go to the river and be baptized in the name of Jesus Christ." Many people went with him and were immersed in baptism. Ernest explained to Jerome that making a confession of Christ wasn't as important to them as baptism in the Name of Jesus, because that step of faith completely separated them from their former religion. Most of them had a red or black spot, called a *bindi*, on their foreheads. The bindi indicated that they were Hindus, and represented the "third eye of spiritual sight". After they were baptized in the river, they wiped the spot off their foreheads, because they were no longer Hindus. They were newly born again Christians, and wanted to follow Jesus from then on. Jerome didn't go to the river with them, but instead went back to the hotel to sleep. In the morning he was met by three men that told him they had been baptizing people all night.

They went by train to visit three other cities. The bathroom on the train was a small room with just a hole in the floor. They travelled overnight and slept on the train. The bunks were very narrow. There were no blankets or pillows or curtains over the bunks, so Jerome made a pillow with his clothes, and when he woke up during the night, he saw people walking by.

In the three cities only ten to fifteen people attended the meetings, so they went back to Hyderabad and helped in the classrooms during the day. The students all wanted to hear about America. The Lord revealed to Jerome that one of the boys had stomach trouble. When he told him so, Ernest said, "The Lord told Jerome that. " The boy had had several surgeries, but still had the problem. Jerome prayed for him, and he was healed.

People in the meetings were especially blessed with the gift of the word of knowledge the Lord gave Jerome. He would pick out people in the crowd and tell them what was wrong with them. Then he would pray, and the Lord would heal them. One was an associate pastor who was suffering constant pain. He shared his medical history which included two surgeries. When Jerome prayed for him in the Name of Jesus, all pain instantly left him.

In one of the meetings, there was a man with three large growths about three inches across and three-fourths inches high on his abdomen. They were hard and unmoving. Jerome prayed for him, then prayed for many more in the church. When he was finished, the man came back, lifted his shirt, and showed that Jesus had healed him--the growths were completely gone.

When the Lord began healing people, hundreds rushed Jerome, but were only able to reach through the crowds to touch his hand. Two circles of men joined their arms around him to hold back the needy crowds. There was no way to know how many received healings, but Jerome knew he had prayed for hundreds.

The dedication of Dr. Ernest Komanapalli was amazing. He was truly a man of God as he gave his life for the children in the orphanage.

Jerome's experiences in India opened his eyes to the poverty in that nation. But it was a wonderful time of serving the Lord, and knowing that only God could do this.

GREECE

"I walked where the Apostle Paul walked," Jerome reminisced. "What a thrill!" His friends wanted to show Jerome and JoAnn the sights of Athens, and it was the most interesting place he had ever seen. They saw the temple near the Acropolis, where Paul spoke to the Athenians. They went to an area with public baths where there were tunnels, and a river underneath where people could bathe.

They stopped for lunch at a restaurant built on the edge of a cliff. Their booth had glass on one side, and they could look straight down to the bottom. Many people were drinking tea, and there were shops with all kinds of tea--not in bags, just the leaves, and in many different flavors. They bought some, but back home, they couldn't make it taste like the Greeks did.

They met their friends, Themos and Joanna, when Themos was attending Bible College in Seattle. After he earned his degree, he returned to Greece to minister. He had churches in Crete, the island of Rhodes, and Athens. Themos wanted Jerome and JoAnn to visit, so they went in 1994. They stayed at Themos' home on the island of Crete, and Jerome ministered healing in Themos' church.

God revealed the people's problems to Jerome, and they came up for prayer. One man had five growths, three of which were the size of eggs on his chest. Jerome felt them, and prayed for him, but didn't see any difference. He encouraged him to keep believing. An hour later, all of the lumps were gone. What a faith builder for the people!

God spoke to Jerome's mind about a man sitting in the back, who was curled over. Jerome asked him to come forward, and tell him what happened that made him so twisted. He said he was a bull fighter, and was gored by a bull. Jerome placed his hands on each side of his face, and asked him to get his body in motion. As he prayed and the man moved, he got straighter and straighter. Jerome stood back. The man took a few steps, tested his back, and discovered that his body was normal again. The other people witnessed it, and shouted praises to God. Others were healed as well, for God was really moving that evening.

The second night God continued to work miracles. At first the Lord didn't lead Jerome to pray for a young woman with legs swollen all the way to her ankles, but instead went to an older woman at the end of the row. He took her hands, and felt impressed of the Lord to say, "Tonight God will give you the desires of your heart."

She started crying, and then Jerome went back to the girl with the swollen legs and asked her to get up and walk. She did so with great difficulty. He prayed for her, but nothing happened. He prayed again with more fervor, but still nothing. He turned around, still expecting Jesus Christ to do something. As he walked away from her, God started working. He turned around and pointed at her and said, "This girl will walk. This girl will walk. I promise you this."

The next morning, her legs were completely normal. God also gave the older woman the desire of her heart, as He promised. She was the girl's mother, and her desire was that her daughter would be healed.

The next morning, a young college professor came to see Jerome. Because of a car accident, he was paralyzed from the waist down. He was able to get around because of a modified car, and a wheelchair with special controls. He had attended every service, but hadn't been healed. He said, "I know God can heal me." Jerome prayed, prayed again, and prayed a third time, but nothing happened. "Go believing," Jerome said. "God isn't done with you yet."

At the next service he was there in his wheelchair. Jerome was startled when out of his own mouth God spoke through him and said, "This man came to where I am staying, and I prayed for him three times. Nothing happened then, but this man is going to walk out of here tonight."

The professor was fifteen feet away. Two men helped him stand, and a lady handed him some crutches. He stood alone, and the two men sat down. There was silence in the church. Everyone looked at his feet. He moved one foot about three inches forward, then the other three inches. After a third small step, he stopped, put both crutches in his left hand and walked the rest of the way to Jerome. The congregation was overjoyed to see God heal him. They all knew he had been paralyzed for several years.

The next day they went to the island of Rhodes, "the Pearl of the Mediterranean Sea". Mainland Turkey is so near, it can be seen from Rhodes. A threat to Greece, a mountain was equipped with big guns pointed toward Turkey in case they invaded. The Greeks didn't get along with Turkey. In fact, Turkey didn't get along with any of its neighboring countries.

Many of the church people from Crete also came to Rhodes for the service that night. After that one service, Jerome and JoAnn went to Athens, where Themos and Joanna showed them the sights.

Jerome ministered in a large church in Athens. Besides people from Athens, some travelled two hundred seventy miles from Rhodes and Crete to attend the meeting.

At the end of their trip, Themes wanted prayer for all the elders of his churches, so Jerome prayed for them, even though it took all his strength. He was so tired and weak that he started speaking strangely, passed out, and fell on the floor. They found a chair for him to sit on, and they held up his arms as he prayed. He was extremely tired, but God held him together. From Athens JoAnn and Jerome went home.

For JoAnn and Jerome as well as for Paul centuries before them, it was obvious that only God could do this.

RUSSIA

"This man was dead"--words written at the end of 15 feet of paper running through an EKG machine. No heartbeat had shown for quite some time, so the doctor made that assessment, wrote those words on the paper, and began to unhook the patient from the machine. Jerome was the patient, in a hotel in Siberia.

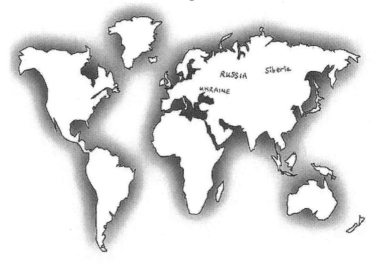

He has had so many heart attacks and strokes throughout his life that he has lost count. Having one close to home is one thing. Having one of each half way around the world is another. Not only was there the problem of getting good professional medical help; there was also the matter of getting back home alive.

Jerome made several evangelistic trips with his partner, Don Van Paris. Don was with him in the Ukraine when he had a stroke, and later on a different trip, a heart attack. JoAnn was always fearful of

Jerome travelling so far away from home, but Don assured her that he would get him home safely. It was a promise he was determined to keep.

In 1995 in a rural area near Kiev in the Ukraine, people came out of the fields to a church to hear him speak. They were hungry for God, and as Jerome spoke, the presence of the Spirit of the Lord and His compassion for them was unmistakable. When it was time to pray for the sick, many people with injuries and sicknesses came forward. Some were lame; many had back problems; one lady was blind in one eye. Many of the back problems were caused by one leg being shorter than the other. As Jerome prayed for them, the short legs lengthened, and the back pain ceased. The blind lady regained her sight.

After that meeting the Pastor set up a meeting for them in another rural area, six hours away. Kiev roads were very rough, and they couldn't go any faster than 25 -30 mph. Two Ukrainians drove, and on the way, the tail pipe of the car fell off. They stopped the car, wondered what to do, cut off some wire from the speaker for the radio, wired the exhaust pipe up, and were on their way again.

When they arrived at their destination, a little town out in the country, the people warmly greeted them. Before the meeting in their big church, they gave Jerome, Don and the drivers a meal, after which Jerome had a stroke, couldn't move his arm and became nearly unconscious. He rested at one of the resident's houses that evening, while Don preached, and the Lord performed many miracles.

Right after the meeting Don knew he had to get Jerome back to the United States for treatment, but things in that area did not happen quickly. They put

Jerome in the front seat with the Ukrainian driver, and took off in the dark driving across country. Jerome didn't even know what was happening.

Halfway back to Kiev a car with KGB men turned on their siren, and pulled them over. One man stood in front of the headlights with a submachine gun strapped over his shoulder, and a pistol in his hand. Another guard came up with the same equipment, told Don to get out of the car, and give them his passport. The guards thought Jerome was sleeping. Then the Ukrainians and the guards started arguing. Don later said, "Since I didn't know the language, I didn't know what was going on. I didn't know if it was our Waterloo, time to meet the Lord, or what." It turned out the guards and the Ukrainians were arguing about money. Don gave them some, and they travelled on.

By the time they got into Kiev, Jerome was quite ill. The Pastor took him to a home owned by a massage therapist, who massaged Jerome's head, which gave him some relief from the pain. They had no flight reservations, so they had to stay there for three days until Don could make arrangements. Jerome refused to go to the hospital. He just wanted to get on an airplane and get back to Seattle. Eventually they were able to fly to Moscow, then transfer to a plane for Seattle.

Jerome was awake, but he couldn't speak. In Moscow they wanted to take him to a hospital, but he shook his head "no". On the way to Seattle, he got worse, so Don asked the flight attendant for oxygen. Instead she found a doctor on board. The doctor checked him over, and told her that they should turn the plane around and go back to Russia. Jerome and

Don refused, so the doctor returned to his seat, drank heavily, soon fell into a deep sleep, and didn't realize five hours had passed. He awoke and went to check on Jerome, who was now comatose. He again said that they should turn the plane around and return to Russia. Don reasoned with him, pointing out that they were five hours into a nine hour flight. They were closer to Seattle than to Moscow, so the doctor was content. Jerome revived enough to go out in a wheelchair upon arrival in Seattle, and Don was able to get him home to bed.

As Jerome lay there in bed, he received a vision from the Lord. In the vision he saw a red horizon, and in it there was a red bowl, which turned to green, and then faded away. Then a star came down to him, and it began to open like petals on a flower. Inside there was a pearl, the size of a basketball. Years later as he was laying on his bed listening to Christian music, he saw the red horizon come over him again, and the Lord spoke to him: "You died," He said. Then the green appeared to go all over him. "But I have more for you to do." Then he saw the pearl and the Lord said, "I am pleased with your life."

On another trip they went to Ufa, Siberia. A woman named Olga interpreted for them, and with her help they spoke in several churches. One evening they ministered in an opera house to a large crowd, but during the meeting, Jerome had a heart attack and became quite weak. Don suggested that he give Jerome's testimony for him, and then Jerome could pray. They followed that plan, and the Lord greatly anointed Jerome to pray for many.

One was a young boy that came forward limping with a deformed foot, and was instantly healed by the Lord. Jerome asked if he could keep his cane, but the boy refused. He wanted to mount the cane on his wall, to show what Jesus had done for him.

As he prayed for many others, Jerome became weaker and weaker. Don called the team members together, Jerome laid his hands on each of them, and asked the Lord to continue the healing work through them. They prayed for nearly an hour, and saw God work many miracles through them. In the meantime Jerome was taken to a back room with a chair and a desk. Jerome sat on the chair, put his head on the desk and passed out. After the service the van driver tried to help him stand, but after taking four steps he fell on the floor. He had no pulse and he wasn't breathing. Don didn't think he should do CPR because Jerome had asked him not to do anything "heroic", so he just prayed and rebuked the spirit of death, and Jerome started breathing. On the trip to the hotel, the same thing happened. With prayer the spirit left again, and the Lord caused Jerome to breathe.

Jerome told Don, "I'm not going to make it. I have $1000 in my pocket. I want you to take it and get my body home." To which Don replied, "I don't need your money. You're not going to die."

Foreigners who were sick were not allowed in the hotel, so the team decided to say that Jerome was drunk—a common occurrence in Siberia. Don told Olga to go in and keep the elevator door open. As Don and Jerome approached the hotel door, a guard with a gun stood right in front of them. Don shoved him aside, then moved right past him and the hotel manager, and took Jerome up to his room. The pastor of the church called a member of his congregation, a cardiologist, to come to the hotel. She wasn't allowed to come as a doctor, because Jerome was not a resident in her section of the city. So she and her assistant posed as prostitutes.

She was able to smuggle in an EKG machine in her suitcase, and hooked Jerome to it. She determined that he had a carotid pulse. Jerome stopped breathing again, his heart beat three times, and then the line made by the EKG machine flat lined for 15 feet of paper.

All the while Don prayed, calling on the name of Jesus. The doctor injected medication into his heart, but it didn't do anything. She thought it was over, so she wrote on the paper, "This man was dead." Just as she was about to shut off the machine, she saw one little bleep, a slight mark from the flat line--then another and another. His heartbeat grew stronger and stronger, and Jerome revived.

That morning as soon as he was able, Don got him to the airport, and found a wheelchair for him. The line through customs was quite long, and the room was terribly hot. Don wheeled the chair up to the front of the line and told the official, "This man is sick, and needs to get into a cool building." They were told they could, and went quickly through customs. Jerome said, "Well we're free now. We've made it through customs."

"No," Don replied. "We won't be free until we touch down in the U.S." He had no sooner said that when a guard that apparently didn't know English motioned to Don to follow him. He left Jerome and followed the guard down a dark tunnel underneath the airport. It was rather frightening for Don, and Jerome didn't know where he had gone. The guard and Don followed a string of small lights, until they found Jerome's luggage, in which were a couple of swords that Jerome had purchased. The guard needed to check the swords for drugs. He took a piece of metal and tapped it all the way down each sword. Then in perfect English he said, "I'm sorry to put you through this, but I had to check."

Don exclaimed, "You speak perfect English!" To which the guard replied, "You catch on fast!"

In the meantime, word had gotten back to the states that Jerome had had a heart attack in Russia. Christians all over the Seattle area, and perhaps beyond were praying fervently for him. Our gracious God and Savior heard and answered those prayers and got him home safely again.

Jerome made several trips with Don Van Paris. They didn't know the languages, and they were in some dangerous situations, but the Lord always watched over them, kept them safe, met their needs, and demonstrated that only God could do this.

AFRICA

For nearly three weeks in August and September of 1996, Jerome travelled with Mike Dilio and Roger Sonnesyn half way around the world and back, through a region plagued by war, poverty, witchcraft and disease, successfully ministering to thousands of Africans in difficult settings, and because of the Lord's mercy and protection, not once were they in danger. Daily they were blessed by the prayers of friends and families back home, as well as the care given them by the brothers and sisters in the Full Gospel Businessmen's Fellowship of East Africa.

The first part of the Airlift was to Uganda. Ron and Shirley De Vore hosted them for nine of the seventeen days of their trip. Ron was an old timer with the FGBMFI who answered the Lord's call to fulltime missionary work. The De Vores made them feel right at home and treated the team like royalty.

In Uganda they focused on prison ministry. They were led by the Lord into four separate prisons to share testimonies of salvation along with Jerome's graceful healing ministry. They prayed for about six hundred fifty prisoners, led one hundred twenty-six to a decision for Christ, and prayed for healing. In one prison the Director was also saved.

Ron and Shirley drove them past the head waters of the Nile River to the northern region of the country where there had been terrible war devastation, in order to meet their Bellevue chapter sponsored orphan, Epecu. He was overwhelmed as were all the Christians in the village to have unexpected visitors from America. They had a blessed time together, and the team was motivated to help many more needy children with scholarship money to help pay for school fees.

One evening they met with the leaders of the Kampala Chapter to discuss ways to build up and promote the Full Gospel Businessmen's Fellowship in

Uganda. They discovered that some of the issues they faced at home were the same as those in Kampala. They prayed together and fellowshipped as brothers, hoping to work together in the future as partners in the ministry.

Then on to Rwanda. The team was aware of terrible intertribal conflicts there, but had no idea of the evidences of the horrors they were about to witness — memorials to the genocidal attempt to eliminate a whole tribe, the Tutsis. An estimated eight hundred thousand men, women and children were slaughtered in one hundred days in 1994.

The first day in Rwanda for the team was incredibly blessed by the brothers and sisters of the Full Gospel Fellowship. After barely settling into their rooms, they were whisked away for a power packed and anointed prayer meeting. The people spoke the local Kinyarwanda language, so the team needed a translator with them. They were greeted as brothers from America and asked to explain why they were there. The team said the Lord sent them to minister humbly to the brothers and sisters who had suffered so much, and to bring them healing from Jesus. They all smiled and continued to pray together for a successful Airlift. There was a sweet spirit with singing, testimonies and praises offered to God like at Full Gospel Businessmen's meetings in the United States.

The team was surprised to find ten active chapters of the Fellowship in Rwanda, even though they had just begun the previous year. They were inspired to see how convinced the Rwandans were about the power of the Holy Spirit. Membership was growing fast.   Word was out among the business and professional people that the FGBMFI meetings were not just "playing church". In a country devastated by church officials involved in the genocide, the FGBMFI offered a welcome relief from church politics mixed up in tribal matters.   In these simple Full Gospel meetings, the Rwandans experienced powerful anointing and the Lord's presence. By Jesus' power people's tattered lives were healed, there was refreshing from daily suffering, and broken relationships were mended.

The next day they were guests at a breakfast banquet, with a chance to encourage the leaders of the chapters of the capital city and to minister in healing. Mike and Roger shared about their lives walking with Jesus. Jerome told of miracles, how the Lord saved his life many times, and how God was there for healing that morning. It was just what they needed to hear. About ten people received Jesus as Lord of their lives, and then Jerome prayed for healing.   The response was amazing. There was a line of people stretching all the way around the room and Jerome prayed for two hours nonstop, with Jesus healing every kind of illness and problem.

That afternoon they and several Rwandans, travelled in a hired van to one of the many sites that existed around the country as memorials of the genocide. A difficult experience for Americans; a more difficult one for Rwandans, reminding them of the nightmare that deeply traumatized them. The site, a former parish church, was near the capital in a predominantly Tutsi tribal area called Ntarama. It was a horrible scene.

Shattered stained glass windows, and walls completely blown out was all that was left of the church; the inside strewn with the tattered remains of murdered men, women and children. In their imaginations they could hear machine gun bursts and grenades mixed with the prayers of the victims. Overwhelming odors prevented them from getting too close. Skulls and bones of several victims were on the altar. Outside the church was a covered tent with long tables containing more bodies, piled in a horrific display of bones and blood stained clothes.

A local woman with a large towel wrapped around her head stood not far away, and they asked her to tell them what had happened there. She described what she had seen, with the help from the translator.

"One night the army arrived in two troop transport vehicles and went from house to house killing everyone. Those who fled sought sanctuary in this church. After several days the army and other trained "interhamwe" or militia attacked the church and started killing everyone. Many ran into the swamp to hide some miles away but the soldiers continued to hunt them. Not many escaped. I was hit from behind with a club. The blow caused part of my scalp to pull forward over my face. I was knocked unconscious, and left for dead. When I regained consciousness, I pulled my scalp back, and wrapped my head in a towel. Then I found the murdered body of my husband. I'm staying here. This is my home". The team prayed for her, and gave her some money.

The van passed another mass grave site with hundreds of crosses placed in rows marking the bodies of young and old, mostly women and children. No one in the van spoke on the way back to the capital.

In the late afternoon they stopped to see one of the orphanages that housed two hundred children up to the age of ten. There were many such places — there were many orphans. An attempt was made by the administrators to find the parents of the children or to place them in a Rwandan family. The facilities and resources were meager, but the children seemed happy. The director was a strong Christian man and one of the Full Gospel Chapter leaders. He had soft, caring eyes, but it was difficult for him to cope with so much responsibility with so little resources. He told the team that sometimes he just cried for them.

The following day the team went to a University town, Butare, where they were again invited to a banquet by the budding chapter there. It was uplifting to see college students witnessing for Jesus, praising Him publicly, singing songs and dancing for joy because of what Jesus had done for them. The team gave an opportunity for salvation and some responded. Again Jerome was used in a great healing ministry. The team drove all the way back to Kigali praising and singing Rwandan songs about the Lord, Jesus.

Nkusi Josias did a masterful job planning the itinerary, but he told them that to get into one of the prisons to minister to those involved in the genocides would be difficult. The government was very sensitive about international publicity regarding those arrested for acts of genocide, but the Lord made a way for the team to visit the big maximum security prison in Kigali. As they entered they heard a loud commotion, which the Director of the prison said was the aftermath of a riot that had happened earlier that morning. No one had been seriously hurt, but the intense emotions of the prisoners could be felt. The team was concerned, but prayed and decided to trust God.

They stepped up onto a wooden platform about three feet high, and as they did, a sudden peace flooded the yard. The team shared their testimonies about their personal Lord who died so that everyone might have a new life. They told them that new life in Jesus means just what it says. There are no qualifications; it applies to everyone. They recalled Jesus' parables of the lost sheep and the prodigal son.

As they spoke a very powerful spiritual anointing came down. They asked for those who wanted to receive Jesus, and estimated that eight hundred men raised their hands to choose Jesus as their new Master and Savior. It was truly amazing grace. Before they departed, Jerome led the group in prayer for healing. What a thrill to see men like these, smiling and praising God for new life and healing! They praised God with dancing, singing, hugging each other, and talking about Jesus.

It was a successful airlift: hundreds gave their lives to Jesus and hundreds received healings from the Lord; students and orphans gained new sponsors; many were baptized in the Holy Spirit; a new church was started; many received Bibles; God Almighty demonstrated love, fellowship and genuine caring through the team.

Truly, only God could do this.

EPILOGUE

God cares about the whole of us, and heals our bodies when we believe in Him. But His greatest concern is that we live with Him for all eternity. Physical healings are only temporal. Eventually healed bodies die. As King David said in Psalm 23, "Yea though I walk through the valley of the shadow of death. . ." But our ultimate hope is to "dwell in the house of the Lord forever."

Life on this earth is a testing ground for life after death — either joyful eternal life with Jesus, or tortured eternal death, separated from God. When Jerome nearly died of acute nephritis, he was headed for eternal death, and it terrified him. But when he accepted Jesus Christ as his Lord and Savior, and totally lived for Him, he found abundant life on this earth, and assurance of life after death.

Through these testimonies, you can see that miracles didn't cease at the end of Bible times. "Jesus Christ is the same yesterday, and today and forever." (Hebrews 13:8) The same God that healed Jerome, and worked through him to heal countless others, is available to you, whatever your physical circumstances. God is speaking to you, giving you hope. He has no favorites. He loves **you**.

We pray that this little book has blessed you. If you are a discouraged Christian, look up! The Almighty God who made you, is watching over you. Just cry out to Him. As you "abide in the vine" (John 15:5), as Jerome does, you will also find peace, healing, and God working all things together for your good, because you love Him. (Romans 8:28)

If you don't know Jesus as your personal Savior, you can begin your walk with Him right now. Just put this book down and talk to Him. Ask Him to forgive everything you have done that displeases Him. Then dedicate yourself to live fully for Him. He will forgive you, and give you a new life. It's not too late! You haven't committed the unpardonable sin. If God can save despicable criminals, he can save you, too.

If you are a victorious Christian, praise the Lord! Keep abiding in the vine, and we'll look forward to meeting you on the other side!

And always remember. . .only God could do this.

If you wish to contact Jerome, you may send him an e-mail: OnlyGod7@outlook.com

36912531R00046

Made in the USA
Middletown, DE
14 November 2016